Amanda Gorman's

Biography.

Biography of the Poet Laureate, Activist and Model. Author of Change Sings and The Hill we Climb…

TABLE OF CONTENTS

INTRODUCTION

There is a lot of buzz around that beautiful young African-American lady in a yellow suit that stood on the podium and recited a poem for the entire world in the inauguration of the U.S President, Joe Robinette Biden. Her name is **Amanda Gorman**.

Amanda Gorman first made history in 2017 when she became the first National Youth Poet Laureate in the United States. She also made another history on 20th January 2021, when she recited her poem, *The Hill We Climb*, at the Presidential inauguration event in front of millions of viewers across the globe, making her the youngest poet laureate to speak at a U.S Presidential inauguration ceremony. This is a feat stamped in the history books and will be talked about by generations to come.

Many people are curious to know more about this young poet, who was given a mic on such a momentous occasion, or—depending on when reading this—who gave a speech at the Super Bowl LV event.

Well, in the next few pages, you will know more about Amanda S.C Gorman.

Amanda Gorman, an American poet and activist, is from Los Angeles, California. She is an award-winning *cum laude* graduate from Harvard with a B.A in Sociology. Her catalog stems across issues of marginalization, oppression, police brutality, feminism, racism and abortion bans, and the incarceration of migrant children.

In 2014, she founded a non-profit organization, *One Pen One Page,* that centers around supporting youth advocacy, leadership development, and poetry workshops.

In 2015, she, with the help of Urban Word LA, published the book, *The One for Whom Food Is Not Enough.* Her poem, *The Hill we Climb,* which was recited at U.S President Joe Biden's inauguration ceremony, has gotten global recognition and has invigorated two of her books to reach Bestseller status. This has opened doors for many professional management contracts.

She is the youngest Inaugural Poet in the whole of U.S history.

Let's delve deeper into the upbringing of this amazing lady.

Early Life

Amanda Gorman was born on 7 March 1998. She has a twin sister, Gabrielle Gorman, and an elder male sibling. Gabrielle is an activist and Filmmaker.

Amanda and her siblings were raised in West Los Angeles, California, by their single mother, Joan Wicks, a sixth-grade Math and English teacher in Watts.

Gorman always referred to her younger self as a 'weird child' that enjoyed reading and writing and was greatly encouraged by her mother. She often stated that she grew up in an environment with less access to television.

She and her sister Gabrielle grew up with a childhood speech impediment. It's an auditory processing disorder, which makes one very sensitive to sound. She had trouble pronouncing some letters in the alphabet, e.g., the Letter R. She would prefer to say "Women are brilliant," rather than "Girls are smarter," just to evade the 'R.'

Amanda had to take part in speech therapy when she was younger. However, she once said she doesn't view her speech impediment as a setback; rather, she sees it as a gift and her strength because as she was experiencing these obstacles in terms of her speech, it helped her to become really good at reading and writing.

She practiced a lot with the Hamilton song, *Aaron Burr*, because it is packed with Rs. According to Gorman, if she could keep up with Leslie on that track, then she was on her way to being able to say this *R* in her poems.

Gorman attended a private school in Santa Monica called *New roads for grades K-12*. In Second grade, she performed a monologue in the voice of Chief Osceola Florida Seminole's tribe.

She became Keen on poetry when her third-grade teacher read Ray Bradbury's *Dandelion Wine* to the class.

When she was a senior, she received a college scholarship from the Milken family foundation. She went on to Harvard University in Cambridge, Massachusetts, USA, where she studied sociology and graduated in 2020 with honors, as well as many awards. She was a *Phi Beta Kappa* member.

Her Parents

Not much is known about Amanda's parents at this time, especially her dad. Remember she was raised by her single mother, Joan Wicks, and these are the facts we have about her:

Asides from being a 6th-grade teacher, Wicks received her B.S. in Communicative Disorders from Northwestern University and a Master's degree in School Leadership for Social Justice at Loyola Marymount University (LMU), where she also bagged certificates in special education (SEN) and charter school leadership.

According to her resource page online long since last updated, she was in the process of gaining her doctorate at LMU, so we're guessing she must have obtained this.

Her interests span from writing, research, technology, dance, tennis, golf, etc.

Career

2013

Gorman's art and activism are deep-rooted in issues centered around feminism, marginalization, oppression, race, and how it affects the African diaspora.

She stated that watching the Pakistani Nobel Prize Laureate Malala Yousafzai's Eloquent Speech was what inspired her to become a 2014 youth delegate for the United Nations.

2014-2015

In 2014, Gorman was appointed the National Youth Poet Laureate of Los Angeles. She was only 16 at the time, and notable sources said she was in the middle of editing the first draft of a novel she started writing two years earlier.

She finally published the poetry book titled *The One for Whom Food Is Not Enough* in 2015.

2016

In 2016, Gorman became the founder of a non-profit organization, *One Pen One Page* that encourages youth writing and leadership programs.

2017

In April 2017, while Gorman was still studying at Harvard, she became the first person to be named National Youth Poet Laureate. She was selected from five finalists. Gorman also became the first youth poet to open the literary season for the library of Congress. That same year, she became the first author to feature in XQ institute's *Book of the Month*.

For her September performance at the library of Congress, she wrote *In This Place: An American Lyric,* which memorialized the Inauguration of Tracy K. Smith as a Poet Laureate of the United States.

She was presented with a book deal to write two children's picture books by *Viking Children's Books*. She also wrote a tribute to black athletes for *Nike*. She read her Poem on *MTV*.

Gorman also won a $10,000 grant from *OZY*, in the OZY Genius Award, in which students from 10 different colleges are giving the opportunity to pursue their innovative visions and ideas.

Gorman said she'd love to run for President in 2036, and she is keen on pursuing that vision.

2018

When Gorman was selected as one of the *College Women of the Year* by Glamour Magazine, she revisited her views and hopes of becoming President someday. She went further to talk about ways in which she, being a young black woman, can inspire people and affirmed her interest in politics. She said, "I don't want to just speak words: I want to turn them into realities and action."

In 2018, Gorman's *In This Place: An American Lyric* poem was acquired by Morgan Library and Museum, and it was displaced very close to Elizabeth Bishop's works.

2019

In 2019, Gorman was featured in The Root Magazine's *Young Futurist*. It's an annual list of 25 best and brightest young African-Americans who performed exceedingly well in the fields of social justice and activism, enterprise and corporate innovation, art and culture, science and technology, and green innovation.

2020

In 2020, Gorman put forth another amazing poem that focused on climate crisis, and she titled it *Earthrise*.

She also had the opportunity to meet Oprah Winfrey virtually when she featured on an episode of *Some Good News*, the web series hosted by John Krasinski, where she issued virtual inception for those who could not be present for the commencement due to the Covid-19 pandemic in the U.S.

2021

Gorman's recitation of her *The Hill We Climb* poem at the U.S Presidential inauguration ceremony on January 20, 2021 is one of the major highlights of her career. Her being the youngest poet to ever read at a presidential inauguration in the United States makes it steal the show when you get to that page on the United States' History Book.

Gorman got a chance to recite her piece at the Presidential inauguration ceremony because Dr. Jill Biden, the *46th First Lady of the United States*, recommended her. Biden became a fan after experiencing the young and talented Amanda at the Library of Congress in Washington, D.C., USA, on September 13, 2017, when she recited the poem, *In This Place (An American Lyric)*.

Gorman said her inspiration for the poem *The Hill We Climb* came about while she was watching the news about how supporters of then-President Donald Trump breached the U.S. Capitol in Washington, D.C., on January 6, 2021. She wrote and amended the poem's wording to address the storming of the Capitol that day.

On the Inauguration day, she wore a pair of earrings and a ring, which was given to her as a gift from Oprah Winfrey, as she recited her poem.

After Gorman's performance at the inauguration, two upcoming poetry books of hers, the poetry collection of *The Hill We Climb*, and a project for kids, *Change Sings: A Children's Anthem*, ranked at the top section of *Amazon's Bestseller list*. The Two books, according to Gorman, are scheduled to be released in September 2021. The book version of *The Hill We Climb* is scheduled to be released on March 16, 2021, featuring Oprah Winfrey at the foreword, and it's believed that each of Gorman's three upcoming books will have estimated first printings of one million copies. *Wow!*

After her Inaugural speech, Hillary Clinton made a tweet in support of Gorman's 2036 presidential aspirations.

She was commissioned to compose and recite an original poem at the February 7, 2021 Super Bowl LV's pregame ceremony to serve as the introduction to the three honorary captains that would preside over the coin-toss.

WME and its branch company, IMG Models, have assigned Gorman as a representation for their brand in fashion, beauty, and talent endorsements, announced on Twitter. She also has notable brands like the *Writers House, Gang, Tyre, Ramer, Brown & Passman law* firm representing her in the publishing industry.

Personal Life

Gorman is a parishioner at St. Brigid Catholic Church in Los Angeles. She once got a standing ovation for performing her poem to the parishioners at St. Brigid, but this was long before her burst into the limelight.

Gorman highlights Maya Angelou, Ron Chernow, Toni Morrison, and J.K. Rowling as her favorite authors. She also put Toni Morrison and Yusef Komunyakaa among her artistic influences.

Notable Presence and Recognitions

St. Brigid Catholic Church.

Gorman identifies as a Black Catholic that attends St. Brigid Catholic Church, Los Angeles.

Milken Family Foundation.

Gorman received a College scholarship from the *Milken family foundation* when she was a senior.

Harvard University.

Amanda Gorman went to Harvard University in Cambridge, Massachusetts, USA, where she studied sociology, and graduated in 2020 with honors.

Youth Poet Laureate of Los Angeles

In 2014, Amanda Gorman was chosen as a youth Poet of Los Angeles.

The One for Whom Food Is Not Enough

In 2015, *Urban World LA* helped Gorman publish her poetry book, *The One for Whom Food Is Not Enough*.

One Pen One Page.

Gorman founded a nonprofit organization named *One Pen One Page* that encourages and assists youth writing and leadership programs.

The Library of Congress.

In September 2017, Amanda Gorman recited her poem *In This Place (An American Lyric)* at the Library of Congress during the Inauguration of Tracy K. Smith as Poet Laureate of United States in Washington, D.C., USA. It's also where Dr. Jill Biden discovered her.

Book of the Month (XQ institute)

In 2017, Gorman became the first featured author on XQ Institute's *Book of the Month.*

Nike

In 2017, Gorman wrote a tribute for black athletes for *Nike.*

Viking Children's Book.

Amanda Gorman had a book deal with *Viking Children's Books* to write two children's picture books in 2017.

MTV

Gorman read her poem on *MTV* in 2017.

National Youth Poet Laureate

In April 2017, while Gorman was at Harvard, she became the first person to be named *National Youth Poet Laureate*.

OZY Genius Awards.

Gorman won a $10,000 grant from media company *OZY* in 2017.

Glamour magazine.

Amanda Gorman was selected as one of the *College Women of the Year* by Glamour Magazine in 2018

Morgan Library and Museum.

In 2018, *Morgan Library and Museum* acquired Gorman's poem, *In This Place (An American Lyric)* and displayed it very close to Elizabeth Bishop's works.

The Harvard Crimson.

In 2018, Elida Kocharian of *The Harvard Crimson* wrote about Gorman not viewing her speech impediment as a clutch but more of a gift and a strength.

The Harvard Gazette.

In 2018, Gorman told *The Harvard Gazette* that she always saw her speech impediment as a strength because ever since she started to experience those obstacles in terms of her auditory and vocal skills, she became really good at reading and writing.

Root Magazine (Young Futurist).

In 2019, Gorman was selected as one of The Root magazine's *Young Futurists*, an annual list of *the 25 best and brightest young African-Americans*.

Washington Post.

The week of the inauguration, Gorman told Ron Charles, The Washington Post book critic, "My hope is that my poem will represent a moment of unity for our country," and "with my words, I'll be able to speak to a new chapter and era for our nation."

Some Good News:

In May 2020, Gorman was featured in an episode of the web series, *Some Good News* hosted by John Krasinski, where she was graced with the opportunity of meeting Oprah Winfrey virtually.

Earthrise

In 2020, Gorman released a poem titled *Earthrise*, which focused on the climate crisis.

46th Presidential Inauguration (The Hill we Climb).

In January 2021, Gorman recited her poem, *The Hill we Climb*, at President Joe Biden's Inauguration ceremony.

CBS This morning.

Before her performance, Gorman told Anthony Mason, *CBS This Morning* co-host, that one of the preparations that she does whenever she performs is that she says a mantra to herself, which is "I'm the daughter of black writers. We're descended from freedom fighters who broke through chains and changed the world. They call me."

Amazon Best Seller's List

Gorman's books and poetry collection, *The Hill We Climb*, and a project for youth, *Change Sings: A Children's Anthem*, rank at the top section of Amazon Best Seller's List after her inaugural poem recitation.

IMG Models.

On January 26, 2021, Amanda Gorman signed with *IMG Models*, the international modeling agency, and it was announced on Twitter.

Super Bowl LV pregame.

Gorman composed an original poem that was recited at the Super Bowl LV pregame on Sunday, 7th February 2021.

U.S Presidential Run 2036.

In 2017, Amanda Gorman shared light on her interest in running for President in 2036. Hillary Clinton made a tweet in support of Gorman's 2036 aspiration in January 2021.

TIME

In the 2021 issue of *TIME* titled "The Black Renaissance," Amanda Gorman was the magazine cover.

CONCLUSION

Amanda isn't an overnight success, as you already know. However, being an introvert, not too much is known about her yet. In due time, more details, such as her relationship will be made public, unless she chooses to keep it private, which we will have to respect.

She is of the Pisces sign; no wonder she's so darn creative and imaginative. She has a lot to offer, and we're definitely looking forward for what's ahead in the life and career of Amanda S.C Gorman.

If you enjoyed with biography, kindly leave an honest review - even if you didn't find it interesting that much. Criticism is always welcomed.

Find more Biographies like this on the Amazon author page of **Cypriana Dumm.**

Best wishes.

Made in the USA
Las Vegas, NV
28 March 2021